BEING SAFE AT SCHOOL

BY SUSAN KESSELRING • ILLUSTRATED BY DAN McGEEHAN

The Child's World®

Published by The Child's World®
1980 Lookout Drive • Mankato, MN 56003-1705
800-599-READ • www.childsworld.com

ACKNOWLEDGMENTS
The Child's World®: Mary Berendes, Publishing Director
The Design Lab: Design and production
Red Line Editorial: Editorial direction

LIBRARY OF CONGRESS CATALOGING-IN-PUBLICATION DATA
Kesselring, Susan.
 Being safe at school / by Susan Kesselring;
illustrated by Dan McGeehan.
     p. cm.
 Includes bibliographical references and index.
 ISBN 978-1-60954-300-6 (library bound: alk. paper)
 1. School crisis management—United States. 2. Public schools—
Security measures—United States. 3. Public schools—Safety
measures—United States. 4. Emergency management—United
States. I. McGeehan, Dan. II. Title.
 LB2866.5K49 2011
 363.11'9371—dc22   2010040476

Printed in the United States of America
Mankato, MN
December, 2010
PA02069

About the Author

Susan Kesselring loves children, books, nature, and her family. She teaches K-1 students in a progressive charter school down a little country lane in Castle Rock, Minnesota. She is the mother of five daughters and lives in Apple Valley, Minnesota, with her husband, Rob, and a crazy springer spaniel named Lois Lane.

About the Illustrator

Dan McGeehan spent his younger years as an actor, author, playwright, and editor. Now he spends his days drawing, and he is much happier.

What's the best part of your school day? Is it riding the bus? Maybe it's swinging on the monkey bars at recess. Or do you love solving math problems?

School is a wonderful place to learn and have fun. But you need to watch out for a few things, too. Learn how to be safe and you will enjoy school even more!

Hurry, it's time to catch the bus! Ask a parent to walk you to the bus stop and wait with you. Or, walk with friends. It's best to be with someone you know while waiting for the bus.

At your bus stop, watch out for traffic. Remember to stand on the sidewalk. You'll be safer a few feet away from the street.

Try to be at the bus stop at least five minutes before the bus is scheduled to arrive.

Can your bus driver see you outside the bus? Make eye contact with your bus driver so you know he or she has seen you. When your bus driver opens the doors, you can climb up the stairs into the bus.

If you have to walk in front of the bus to get on, stay five big steps from the bus. Stay two big steps away from the sides—except for when you're getting on and off, of course. And never walk behind the bus. Your bus driver cannot see you there.

Oops! You dropped something by the side of the bus. Just tell your bus driver once you're on your bus. He or she will let you know when it's okay to pick it up.

Once you're on the bus, find a seat right away. Face forward during the ride. Doing so will help keep you safe if there is an **accident**. Keep your feet and school bag out of the middle row where you walk so no one trips. Also, avoid sticking anything out the window. That includes your head and hands!

Your bus driver works hard to get you to school safely. You can help, too. Talk to your friends in a quiet voice. Loud voices can **distract** your bus driver.

If you leave something on the bus, do not go back to get it. Ask your bus driver about it the next time you ride the bus.

Do you like walking to school? It's great exercise and fun, too. Make sure you walk with a friend or a parent. If you ride your bike or scooter, wear a helmet.

Rain or snow can make a walk wet or cold, though. What's your plan for walking in bad weather? Ask your parents what to wear and what to do.

Never let someone give you a ride to or from school unless it is okay with your parents. If a stranger offers you a ride or asks you to get in the car for any reason, stay away from the car. Go straight home or to school and tell an adult.

Your classroom is a pretty safe place to be. But watch out for things that could hurt someone. Keep the floor around your desk clear so your **classmates** won't trip over your things.

Sharp pencils and scissors can poke or seriously hurt someone. Always carry them with the points facing down.

At your desk, sit straight in your chair. Avoid tipping it backward. You could fall and hurt your head.

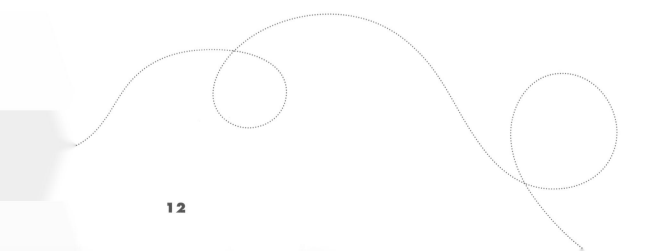

If anyone hits or punches you, tell a teacher right away. But what about mean words? Try to work things out on your own first. If someone hurts your feelings, try to stay calm. Say, "I don't like that," and explain why. If you're the one who hurt somebody else's feelings, apologize. Saying you're sorry takes a lot of **courage**, but you can do it.

It's time for recess! Are you ready to play ball and climb the jungle gym? Jungle gyms are so fun. They've been around for about 90 years! Almost half of all injuries on the playground happen on jungle gyms. That's why it's important to stay safe on the jungle gym and the playground.

If you see something that looks sharp or dangerous, stay away from it. Tell an adult who is outside with you. Avoid touching any animals, such as squirrels or birds. Look out for things you could trip over, too.

17

You've climbed up the ladder. Now you are ready to slide! Remember to wait for the person ahead of you to reach the ground before you go. You don't want to crash into someone! And always slide on your bottom, with your feet in front.

Can you go high on the swings? Just be sure to sit on the seat. Wait until the swing stops before you get off. Also, watch out in front and back of the swings so you don't get kicked.

Only use the playground equipment as it is intended. Only one person should sit on a swing at a time. And only use the ladder to climb up a slide.

The bell is ringing. School's out! All your classmates are ready to leave. You may be in a hurry, but remember to walk. If you run, you could fall or bump someone else.

Tomorrow will be another day to learn and be safe!

SCHOOL SAFETY RULES TO REMEMBER

Always be safe!

1. Wait at the bus stop with a parent or a friend.

2. Make sure your bus driver can always see you when you are outside the bus.

3. Sit quietly on the bus and face forward.

4. If you walk to school, walk with a friend or a parent.

5. Use playground equipment safely.

6. Tell an adult if something happens that hurts or scares you.

7. Move carefully in the classroom, and don't tip your chair.

8. Always walk in school.

GLOSSARY

accident (AK-si-dunt): An accident is something unexpected that happens. In a bus accident, a bus could run into something.

classmates (KLASS-mayts): Classmates are the other children in your class. Be nice to your classmates.

courage (KUR-ij): Courage is bravery. Sometimes it takes courage to apologize.

distract (diss-TRAKT): To distract someone means to interrupt someone who is focusing on something. Do not distract your bus driver while he or she is driving.

TO LEARN MORE

BOOKS

Cuyler, Margery. *Please Play Safe! Penguin's Guide to Playground Safety*. New York: Scholastic Press, 2006.

Knowlton, Marylee. *Safety at School*.
New York: Crabtree Publishing, 2009.

Mattern, Joanne. *Staying Safe on the School Bus*. Milwaukee, WI: Weekly Reader Early Learning Library, 2007.

WEB SITES

Visit our Web site for links about being safe at school:
childsworld.com/links

Note to Parents, Teachers, and Librarians: We routinely verify our Web links to make sure they are safe and active sites. So encourage your readers to check them out!